PHILOSOPHERS OF THE SPIRIT

ECKHART

PHILOSOPHERS OF THE SPIRIT

ECKHART

Edited by

Robert Van de Weyer

Hodder & Stoughton

LONDON SYDNEY AUCKLAND

First published in Great Britain 1998.

The right of Robert Van de Weyer to be identified as the Editor of this
Work has been asserted by him in accordance with the
Copyright, Designs and Patents Act 1988.

1 3 5 7 9 10 8 6 4 2

British Library Cataloguing in Publication Data:
A record for this book is available from the British Library.

ISBN 0 340 69467 X

Typeset in Monotype Columbus by
Strathmore Publishing Services, London N7.

Printed and bound in Great Britain by
Mackays of Chatham PLC, Chatham, Kent.

Hodder and Stoughton Ltd,
A division of Hodder Headline PLC,
338 Euston Road, London NW1 3BH

CONTENTS

SERIES INTRODUCTION

The first task of philosophers is to ask questions – the questions which lurk in all our minds, but which, out of fear or confusion, we fail to articulate. Thus philosophers disturb us. The second task of philosophers is to try and answer the questions they have asked. But since their answers are inevitably only partial, philosophers both interest and infuriate us. Their third and most important task is to stimulate and inspire us to ask questions and seek answers for ourselves.

The human psyche or spirit has always been the main – although not the only – focus of philosophy. And inevitably when the psyche is explored, the gap between religion and philosophy rapidly narrows. Indeed for philosophers in the more distant past there was no gap at all, since philosophy was an aspect of theology and even mysticism. Although religious institutions are now quite weak, questions of spiritual philosophy are being asked more keenly and urgently than ever.

This series is an invitation to readers, with no philosophical training whatever, to grapple with the great philosophers of the spirit. Most philosophy nowadays is served in the form of brief summaries, written by commentators. Each of these books contains an introduction to the life and ideas of the philosopher in question. But thereafter the reader encounters the philosopher's original words – translated into modern English. Usually the words are easy to follow; sometimes they are more difficult. They are never dull, always challenging, and frequently entertaining.

INTRODUCTION

His Genius

Eckhart was a heretic, and near the end of his life was condemned as such; and he was without doubt the most brilliant and subtle heretic of the Middle Ages. At his trial particular phrases and sentences were extracted from his writings and compared unfavourably with orthodoxy. It was a procedure which was grotesquely unfair, as one of the inquisitors – a man who later became pope – acknowledged: a few words, taken out of context, cannot possibly reflect the full meaning of a person's ideas. Eckhart's heresy lay not in specific doctrinal quibbles, but in the entire way in which he approached religious truth. And his ecclesiastical mentors were right to be suspicious of him, since Eckhart's method, taken to its conclusion, undermines the entire purpose of large religious institutions. Yet, if his inquisitors got the better of him in the early fourteenth century, Eckhart is the victor at the turn of the second and third millennia: his approach to truth enjoys a growing appeal today, and arguably offers the only way in which religion can survive and flourish.

Orthodoxy requires people to believe a set of doctrines because those in authority proclaim that they are true. Religion is thus seen in hierarchical terms. At the apex of the hierarchy is God the Father, who chose to reveal himself by sending his Son to be born as a human being. The Son in turn founded an institution, the Church, on which he bestowed his Holy Spirit; and the institution has the task of formulating doctrines, which express in words the truth. The glory of this view of religion is that it is circular and self-confirming: the Church itself asserts this divine hierarchy, which justifies the Church's authority in asserting it.

Eckhart never directly attacked the Church's authority, nor its theological justification. Perhaps, despite his brilliance, he never thought about it; he may unconsciously have feared that, if he did turn his mind to the monstrous edifice, he would have no choice but to knock it down, and hence condemn himself to a heretic's death out of his own mouth. Instead he simply ignored it, and approached truth in his own way. For Eckhart religion is a matter not of what we believe, but of what we perceive; the test of truth is experience. Thus he devoted himself to perceiving the truth for himself; and as a teacher he encouraged and guided others to do the same.

The starting point of his teaching is his distinction between the outer person and the inner person.

The outer person is the body, with its capacity for pleasure and pain, desire and fear. The inner person is the spirit. In most people the outer person dominates the inner: the spirit is being constantly disturbed and upset by the demands of the body. But in order to perceive truth the inner person must become detached from the outer, and become serene and tranquil. To achieve this detachment some people must impose on themselves great hardship and austerity, denying themselves almost all bodily comfort. But for most people moral virtue is the key: suppressing feelings and attitudes which are hateful and negative towards others, and nurturing positive and loving attitudes.

To his orthodox opponents Eckhart's most shocking statements were those describing the consequences of detachment. As you become inwardly more tranquil, you experience the Son being born within the soul. You feel a spiritual light enter you, and a new divine being growing within. Ultimately the Son reaches full stature within the soul, and you are fully united with God. Thus each person is capable of being an incarnation of God, just as the historic Jesus of Nazareth was. Eckhart never appears to have seen the revolutionary consequences of this notion. Firstly, if the position of the historic Jesus is not unique, then the Church's claim to authority collapses. Secondly, if God can become incarnate in every individual, then each individual in whom God's son has been born becomes a possessor and arbiter of truth – and can speak and teach with authority.

Eckhart's primary concern was to nurture the spiritual light in those around him; and his guidance is both practical and at times surprising. He recognises that to most people religion is largely a matter of outward observance and behaviour, such as attending worship regularly, fasting and performing acts of charity. He repeatedly stresses that these activities have no value in themselves. All that matters are our inner motives and intentions. Indeed he says that, if the motive to undertake an action already exists, in God's eyes the action is already fulfilled. Thus, instead of trying to ensure that they behave well, people should keep constant vigil over their thoughts and feelings. If our thoughts and feelings are pure, God will ensure that external consequences fulfil his plan.

It follows from this, and from his general teaching about detachment, that prayer in the normal sense is useless. To ask God for something implies that one is concerned about external matters; and the process of becoming detached means that one must become indifferent. Moreover, prayer suggests that God's will can be changed by human pleading; whereas in truth God in his omniscience must have foreseen the pleading. Thus Eckhart urges people to give up prayer, and instead engage in contemplation, in which the soul dwells on the glory and beauty of God.

Compared with most spiritual writers, Eckhart speaks little about love. This is partly because he fears that in most people's minds it refers to an emotion, which inevitably is transient; whereas to Eckhart love is a matter of will. But this points to a deeper concern. The command that we should love God implies that, by an act of will, we should compel ourselves to love him. In Eckhart's view, while this is laudable, it is even better to compel God to love us. We do this by draining ourselves of all worldly concerns, and thus become empty receptacles – which God in his love must fill. Thus detachment is greater even than love.

Eckhart also speaks surprisingly little about sin. He is acutely aware of the spiritual damage people can do to themselves through an obsession with their own guilt. And he sees that many devout people are constantly trying to placate God through penances of various kinds. He rejects all penances as worthless; and he even suggests that some actions, which we regard as sinful, may in fact be part of God's plan. More profoundly, he believes that obsessive guilt is itself more sinful than any external action, since guilt focuses on the outer self and its failures – whereas the way of detachment requires that the outer person is abandoned.

Today Eckhart is more often referred to as a mystic than as a heretic. In fact his writings show with astonishing clarity why the mystical path tends towards heresy. Mystics seek a direct encounter with divine truth, because they are not content with the verbal formulations of the truth handed down by religious institutions. And many mystics encourage others to join this search, and so undermine those institutions. Eckhart had no intention of undermining the Church, and did not realise he was doing so. But others knew better. They saw in Eckhart a man who followed the mystical path without reserve, going wherever it led; and they saw too a superb teacher, who was taking others with him.

His Life

Just over a hundred years ago a German historian described Eckhart as a 'semi-mythical figure'. The date and place of his birth were unknown, and no record existed of his death. The only certain facts were that he had studied in Paris, that he had held official posts in the Dominican order in Germany, and that he had been condemned as a heretic by a Papal Bull in 1329. The position of his writings was hardly better: a few of his German sermons, which were bound in a volume of another mystic's works, were available to scholars; but the rest of his work had disappeared.

The results of a century of research are astonishing; and both Eckhart and his writings have become familiar to students of spiritual literature. He was born around 1260 in a village in Thuringia called Hochheim, near Erfurt. He may have belonged to a noble family, although this is still a matter of dispute. At around the age of fifteen he was sent to the school which had recently been established in Erfurt, run by the Dominican friars. He soon became a novice of the order, and in 1280 was chosen by his superiors to study theology at Cologne. The Dominicans were usually reluctant to leave their young men at university for a lengthy period, for fear that the freedom of academic life would corrupt them. So he was recalled to Erfurt after one or two years, where he made his final vows as a member of the order.

Probably at around this time he began to preach, both to his own brethren in the friary, and in churches in the surrounding area. His reputation both for eloquence and for intellectual virtuosity quickly spread. In 1293 the order acknowledged his brilliance by sending him to the University of Paris, which was at that time the greatest centre of scholarship in Europe. He spent two years there, beginning his studies for the Master's degree. He was then summoned again back to Erfurt, where he was made prior of the friary; he was also appointed 'vicar' of Thuringia, which meant that he was the senior Dominican in the region. He was an able administrator, and gradually acquired greater responsibilities. In 1303 he was chosen to direct a new division of the order in Saxony; and in 1307 he became vicar of Bohemia. But while these various tasks were time-consuming and arduous, he continued to regard himself primarily as a religious teacher. In the friaries he visited he always spoke to the brethren about spiritual matters; and he willingly preached in nearby churches.

In 1311 Eckhart was again sent to Paris, in order to complete his Master's degree. To attain this rare distinction he wrote a major theological work; and thereafter was always known by the title 'Meister'. He returned to Germany two years later, and moved to Strasbourg, where he spent eight years preaching in the surrounding churches, and giving spiritual direction to several groups of Dominican nuns. He then returned to the university in Cologne, where he had first studied, and was tutor to the most advanced theological students. By now he was without doubt the most popular preacher and teacher in Germany, attracting huge numbers to hear his sermons.

His success evoked increasing jealousy in his more pedestrian contemporaries. The Archbishop of Cologne felt that his own position as the spiritual leader of the city was being usurped; and, in the hope of undermining Eckhart's authority, he urged Eckhart's superiors in the Dominican order to investigate his orthodoxy. The superiors had little choice but to comply; but after a thorough study of Eckhart's publications, they pronounced them free of heresy. The archbishop was dissatisfied with the conclusion, and ordered an inquisitorial investigation. The inquisitors drew up a vast dossier of extracts from his writings and quotations from his sermons, which they claimed controverted orthodoxy; and in 1326 Eckhart appeared before the archbishop and his accusers, formally charged with heresy.

By now Eckhart was an old man, and his powers were waning. He was so indignant about the allegations that he failed to prepare an adequate defence; and he was found guilty. Only then did he consider the case against him in detail, and he prepared a long 'vindicatory document' to demonstrate his innocence. He sent this to the pope, appealing against the archbishop's verdict. He was ordered to appear before the pope in Avignon, and he travelled there in the company of several of his brethren, who staunchly supported him.

By the time he reached his destination he was exhausted, and seriously ill. The proceedings began, but Eckhart was too weak to present his case. Within a few weeks he was dead. Afterwards the pope wrote to the Archbishop of Cologne, claiming that on his deathbed Eckhart had recanted. But the letter contains a qualification, which suggests the recantation was far from total: 'he revoked and deplored his own teachings ... insofar as they could generate in the minds of faithful people a heretical opinion.' In other words, Eckhart did not deny the essence of what he had taught, but merely regretted any damaging consequences.

His Writings

Eckhart died in late 1327 or early the next year. In his lifetime his manuscripts had been widely copied, and many monasteries, convents and churches possessed works by him. But after his condemnation most of these were destroyed. Only a few brave souls dared to keep any of his writings, and during the following century three spiritual authors acknowledged their debt to him. In the sixteenth century a Protestant theologian claimed that Eckhart's ideas foreshadowed those of Martin Luther. Thereafter he and his books disappear from view.

Scholars in the late nineteenth and early twentieth centuries trying to rediscover Eckhart's works faced three formidable problems. Firstly, they had to find in scattered collections of medieval manuscripts those which purported to be by him. Secondly, they had to establish whether Eckhart was indeed the author of any manuscript bearing his name. Thirdly, where several copies of the same work exist, they had to establish which was the earliest and most accurate.

Even now the authenticity and value of many manuscripts are in doubt, and will probably remain so.

Eckhart wrote in both German and Latin, using each language for different purposes. His theological works are mainly in Latin. These are mostly formal and precise, amassing arguments and scoring points, in the style approved by the medieval schoolmen. To the modern reader they are dull and cold, with little to excite the spirit; and his inquisitors found nothing in the Latin texts to which they could object. German is his language for spiritual exploration and for popular teaching; and when he uses his native tongue he throws off the shackles of logic, allowing his mind and pen to follow the movements of his spirit. The inquisitors knew well that heresy is the child of free expression.

The writings contained in this volume are taken entirely from the German corpus. In fact they come mostly from the German works which seem to have emanated directly from Eckhart's hand. *The Talks of Instruction* is probably the oldest of his extant texts, dating from some time prior to 1298. They are probably addressed to friars, although some have suggested that a group of nuns was the original audience. *The Book of Divine Consolation* is the strongest and clearest expression of his mystical doctrines; it appears to have been written in honour of the daughter of the German king, who suffered several bereavements in a short period. The treatise *On Detachment* is the most systematic of his spiritual works, outlining a path which the aspiring mystic can follow. *The Nobleman* is perhaps his most famous sermon, in which he expounds a distinction crucial to his thought, between the outer and the inner person.

In the document vindicating himself which he addresses to the pope, Eckhart wrote of his inquisitors: 'Their mistake lies in thinking that everything they do not understand is an error, and that every error is a heresy.' There are two great attractions in Eckhart's work. Firstly, it is wonderfully clear, lucid and vivid, so that the reader with no religious training can understand its meaning. Secondly, it carries the reader beyond the normal reach of human understanding, towards that realm of truth which can never be expressed in words. His inquisitors not only did not wish to be carried to that realm themselves, but did not want others to go there either. The growing numbers, who in our own time are discovering Eckhart, ride happily on his heretical prose.

ROBERT VAN DE WEYER

FULFILMENT THROUGH REBIRTH

---

from *Sermon on the Just Person*

The just person lives in God, and God lives in the just person. God is born in every virtue of the just person, and is delighted by every virtue; and not only by every virtue, but by every action of the just person, however small it may be ...

The just person does not strive for any rewards. Those who seek a reward are like servants working for a wage, or like those motivated by ambition. If you want to act justly, and become just, do not have any aim or purpose in your actions, either in time or in eternity; do not look for rewards or blessings. Actions with an aim are dead. Indeed, do not even make God your aim; actions intended to satisfy God are dead. Such actions are self-defeating, and are even a form of sin. You would be like a gardener who should have planted a garden, but in fact uprooted all the trees – and then wanted a reward for it. Trying to satisfy God does not satisfy him.

If you want to live, and if you want your actions to live, you must be dead to all things, and you must become nothing. All creatures try to make something out of something; but God's way is to make something out of nothing. So if God is to make any-thing in you or with you, you must first become nothing. Therefore go into yourself, and work there; your actions within yourself will be living ...

In the just person nothing works except God. If any outside stimulus impels you to act, then your actions will certainly be dead. Even if God were to impel you to some external action, that action would also be dead. If you and your works are to live, God must move you in the innermost part of your soul. If you and your works are to live, you must learn to inhabit your soul ...

Sometimes a light appears in the soul, and the person thinks it is the Son; yet it is only a light. When the Son appears in the soul, the love of the Holy Spirit also appears there. It is the nature of the Father to bring the Son into being. It is the nature of the Son that I should be born in him and in his image. It is the nature of the Holy Spirit that I should be burnt in him, and should be completely consumed by him, and become entirely love. Those who are consumed in this way and become entirely love, think that God loves them alone; they think that God does not know anyone else, does not love anyone else, and has not been loved by anyone else.

Some teachers say that the soul is fulfilled through love. Others say that the soul is fulfilled by contemplating God. I say that the soul is fulfilled neither through love, nor in contemplation, nor through visions. You might ask whether the soul has a vision of God in eternal life. But through the very fact of being born the soul has a vision of God. The soul is fulfilled through being born anew where the father lives; that is, through becoming totally simple and totally naked.

So turn away from all distractions, and discover yourself as totally naked. Your outside characteristics are irrelevant; and by thinking about them, you make the soul ask irrelevant questions.

THE CHILD OF GOODNESS

from *The Book of Divine Consolation 1*

You should know that the good person and goodness concern each other and relate to each other in this way. Goodness is not created, nor made, nor born; yet it brings forth – gives birth to – the good person. The good person is born as the child and offspring of goodness, insofar as the good person is truly good. Goodness gives birth to itself, and it comes to birth in the good person. It pours life, knowledge, love and activity into the good person; and the good person receives these qualities from goodness, and from goodness alone. The good qualities and goodness itself are a single entity, in that they exist in perfect harmony ...

There is a second thing you should know, which may bring comfort to you. The just and good person rejoices differently at different events. The good person rejoices far more in observing works of goodness than in any natural human pleasure. For this reason good people gladly give their lives for the sake of justice.

When good and just people suffer external injury, they are not truly troubled; this is because they are in a state of equanimity, and their souls are tranquil. But God may choose to allow injuries to befall those who wish to believe that they are good and just, but are not truly so. In either case people should not resent external injuries, but be glad of them. Injuries enhance human life; and people value their lives more highly than the whole world – because the world would be useless if there was no one to live in it.

The third thing you should know is that in truth God alone is the spring and artery of all goodness, and hence of all knowledge and comfort. Everything that does not come from God brings bitterness, despair and pain; it adds nothing at all to goodness, which comes from God and is God. On the contrary, it diminishes, conceals and hides the sweetness, joy and serenity which God gives.

I shall go further, and say that all true pain comes from external things and their loss. If the loss of eternal things causes me sorrow, this is a sure sign that I love external things – and thus in effect that I love bitterness and despair ... Those who seek joy in external things cannot find joy. But those who love God, and love the presence of God in that which he has created, will find true, full and unending joy.

BORROWING BLESSINGS

from *The Book of Divine Consolation 2*

There is no suffering or loss without some comfort; there is no such thing as sheer loss. We can also find consolation from God, since God and nature can never allow pure evil or pain to exist.

Suppose a man has a hundred marks. He loses forty and keeps sixty. If he constantly thinks of the forty he has lost, he will be filled with despair and resentment. He reflects on his loss and his pain; he pictures his loss in his mind; he looks at it, and it looks at him; he speaks to his loss, and it speaks to him; he and his loss stare at one another. How can he ever be free of sorrow, and receive comfort? But if he were to turn his attention to the sixty marks he still has, looking at his remaining fortune and talking to it, and turn his back on the forty he has lost, he would certainly feel comforted …

When you are suffering and in pain, remember the blessings you still retain. Remember too how many people, if they had the sixty marks which you still possess, would regard themselves as wonderfully happy and truly rich …

I shall make another point: if you have lost a

thousand marks, you should not complain about the thousand marks you have lost. You should thank God, who gave you the thousand marks that you were able to lose – and who allows you, by exercising the virtue of patience, to gain eternal life, which many others will never possess.

There is another thing that may bring comfort. Suppose a man has enjoyed a high reputation and great wealth for many years. Then God decides that he should lose his reputation and wealth. If he is wise, he will thank God. When he becomes aware of the loss and pain he now suffers, he knows for the first time how privileged he was before. He should thank God for that earlier privilege that he enjoyed for so long, even though he never realised his good fortune. On no account should he be resentful. He should remind himself that, on his own merits, he deserves nothing.

We should remember that all good things, and goodness itself, are lent to us by God, not given. God the Father gives the Son and the Holy Spirit everything which is good; he gives no good things to his creatures, but lends good things to them. The sun gives heat to the air, but lends light to it; then, when the sun sets, the air loses its light but retains its heat, because that has been given to the air on its own ...

That is why I say that everything good and pleasurable in the world is lent to us. So we have no right to complain when the one who lent us some good thing wishes to take it back again. We should thank God for lending it to us for so long. We should especially thank God if he does not want the whole of it back.

THE BIRTH OF GOD IN THE SOUL

———————◆———————

from *The Book of Divine Consolation 2*

Inward work – work within the soul – is godly, because it is aimed at making the soul more godlike. Outward work, regardless of its quality and magnitude, its length and its breadth, does not in any way increase the value of inward work. Even in a thousand lifetimes, outward work cannot make a person more similar to God. Inward work is good in itself.

If our inward work is great, it will make our outward work great as well. If our inward work is feeble and worthless, our outward work will be feeble and worthless too. Our inward work draws its goodness from the heart of God, and from nowhere else. It receives the Son into the soul; and the soul is born as a son in the bosom of the heavenly Father. Outward work does not draw goodness directly from God, but receives its goodness from inward work. Outward work is complex, and its value is measured by its quantity; in these respects it is foreign and alien to God. Outward work clings and adheres to inward work, and thus finds serenity and light; but in itself it is blind, without purpose.

Through inward work God's Son is born in the

soul; and the soul is born as a child of God. The Son of God in the soul is the spring and source of the Holy Spirit; and, since God himself is spirit, the Holy Spirit brings to birth God's Son in the soul. God's Son is the origin of all who are children of God; they are born of God, and transformed in his image.

Those in whom God's Son has been born are estranged from all quantity and complexity, including the complexity of the orders of angels. Indeed it is true to say that they are estranged from goodness, truth and everything which allows any shades of difference or distinction. They are entrusted to God, who cannot be received and has no complexity – in whom the Father, the Son and the Holy Spirit are stripped of all differences and attributes, and are totally unified. This unity blesses us.

The further away we are from the unity of God, the less we are children of God, and hence the less perfectly the Holy Spirit springs up in us and flows from us. The nearer we are to the unity of God, the more fully we are children of God, and the more perfectly the Holy Spirit flows from us.

LOVING FOR THE SAKE OF LOVE

from *The Book of Divine Consolation 2*

Good people, or children of God who have been
born in God, love God for his own sake and in himself. Good people have been born in goodness; in
God they have acquired all the properties of God's
nature. One of the properties of God is that he does
all things for himself; he does not look for reasons
outside himself, but only acts for his own sake. He
loves and he acts according to his own nature. Thus
when people love God himself, and when they act
not for reward or honour or happiness, but only for
the sake of God and his glory, that is a sign that they
are children of God.

God loves for the sake of love, and acts for the
sake of action. God could never have brought his Son
into being, unless 'having brought' him into being
were the same as 'bringing' him into being. Thus we
can say that the Father is continually bringing the
Son into being, without interruption. In the same
way, God would never have created the world, unless
'having been created' were the same as 'being created'. Thus God created the world in such a way that
he is continually creating it. The notions of past and

future are alien to God. Therefore those who are born as children of God, love God for his own sake; they love God for the sake of loving him; and they do his work for the sake of doing it.

God never gets weary of loving and acting. And all that he loves is brought into his unity. Thus it is true that God is love.

Good people wish to suffer at all times for the sake of God, and yet at the same time do not want to suffer. While they suffer for God, they feel satisfied; they love suffering for the sake of God and because of God. Good people are children of God, born in him and transformed in his image. Thus they love God for himself. They love God for the sake of love; they do his work for the sake of doing it. Through them God loves and works without interruption. God lives in the feelings and emotions of good people. For good people, the children of God, suffering and working for God's sake brings joy and happiness. The greatest source of happiness is to suffer for God's sake ...

The attitudes and the feelings of our higher nature always bring more happiness and joy than the attitudes and feelings of our lower nature. Normally water flows downhill, since this is natural to it; yet the force of the moon can cause water to forget its nature and flow uphill – as it does when the tide flows. This should indicate to us that, under the force of God's will, we can flow from our lower nature to our upper nature and thereby find greater happiness and joy. Flowing from the lower nature to the upper is what is meant by denying the self and following Christ. If we truly deny ourselves, laying down all selfish concerns, then nothing can cause us sorrow.

God cannot make anyone sad or sorrowful. Therefore those who are children of God, and have been born in him, cannot themselves become sad and sorrowful. When Christ invites us to deny ourselves, take up his cross and follow him, he is not commanding us but making us a promise. He is promising that all suffering – indeed all action – for his sake will bring happiness and joy ...

Ignorant people are often amazed when they see good people suffering. They wonder if the good people's pain and distress are caused by secret sins. They say; 'I thought these people were good. How is it that they now suffer so much?' I agree with them, saying: 'Certainly, if they are truly in distress, and are deeply unhappy, then they are not good people; they are sinners. But if they are good, their suffering brings them great happiness; it is a source of blessing.'

THE POINTLESSNESS OF PRAYER

from *The Book of Divine Consolation 2*

When I was once ill, I was asked why I did not pray to God to cure me. I answered that I had three reasons for not praying to God. Firstly, I was certain that God, who is love, would never allow me to be ill unless it was for my good. Secondly, a good person should accede to God's will, whereas prayer is an attempt to make God accede to the person's will; thus prayer is wrong.

If God wills me to be sick, then I should not want to be well; and if God did not want it, then it would not be so. If God could cure me without willing it, then it would be worthless and undesirable to be made well. Willing comes from love; not willing comes from lack of love. It is much more desirable, and much more beneficial to me, that God should love me and I should be ill, than that I should be physically well and God not love me. That which God loves is something; that which God does not love is nothing ...

The third reason why it would be unworthy and sinful for me to pray to God to cure me is this: I do not want, nor should I want, to ask the powerful, loving, generous God for such a small thing. Let us suppose I travelled a very long distance to see the pope. Then, when I entered his presence, I said: 'My lord, holy father, I have come a long distance on rough roads and at great expense. The reason for my journey is to ask you to give me a bean.' I myself, and anyone who heard me, would quite rightly say that I was a fool. I have no doubt that every creature, and every good that may befall a creature, is smaller in comparison with God than a bean is in comparison with the whole world. So I should rightly despise myself if I – who believe myself to be good and wise – prayed to be cured.

It follows from this that it is a sign of a faint heart to be cheerful or sad on account of the transient things of this world. One should be heartily ashamed before God and his angels, and before other people, to take any notice of them …

THE INNER AND THE OUTER SELF

from *The Nobleman*

Human beings have a twofold nature: body and spirit. In each one of us there is an outer self, and an inner self.

The outer self is involved with the physical aspects of our organs, such as the eye, the ear, the tongue, the hand, and so on. This may be called the original nature, the outward nature, even the hostile and servile nature. It is bound up with the flesh, and clings to the soul.

The inner self may be called the new person, the heavenly person, even the young person. It may also be called 'the nobleman'.

Theologians say that from the moment of birth people have a good spirit, which is an angel, and an evil spirit, which is a devil. The good spirit advises the soul, and constantly urges what is good, divine, virtuous, heavenly and eternal. The evil spirit also advises the soul, and constantly urges what is temporal, transient, wicked, evil and diabolical. The evil spirit converses with the outer self; and through the outer self the evil spirit secretly lies in wait, ready to trap the inner self ... The good spirit is like a seed sown in the field of the human soul. If it is allowed to grow, it brings forth wisdom, knowledge, virtue and goodness. It is the seed of the divine nature, the Son of God, which comes to birth in the soul ...

The first stage in the development of our inner self is when we try to follow the example of good and holy people. The inner person is still like a small child, clinging to chairs in order to stand and walk, and feeding on milk.

The second stage is when we not only follow the external example of good people, but listen to their teaching and their counsel. We turn our back on worldly teaching, and face God. The inner self, as it were, is crawling out of the mother's lap and smiling at the heavenly Father.

The third stage comes when we withdraw ourselves more and more from the mother's care, and are further and further from her lap. We cast off all fear. Even if we were able to do wrong without hurting anyone, we have no desire to do so. We are bound to God by ropes of love. We want only to know more fully the joy, sweetness and bliss which he promises; all else is repugnant to us, because it is alien to him.

The fourth stage is when we put down roots in God's love, and so derive the strength to face all temptations and trials, and endure all pain and suffering, with a glad and willing heart. When we are rooted in God's love, we are constantly joyful, whatever happens to us.

The fifth stage is when we are totally at peace with ourselves in all respects, resting serenely in the richness and fullness of God's wisdom.

The sixth stage is when we are transformed by God, so that we completely conform to his image. We are utterly detached from the transient and temporal things of life, because we are true children of God. There is a stage beyond this; it is the highest stage, where we enjoy eternal peace and joy. Attaining this stage is the fulfilment of the inner self.

We may think of God's image as the seed of God's Son which is sown in the soul. Worldly desire may be seen as earth thrown over the seed, covering it up and preventing it from growing. This mound of desire may be so great that one ceases to be aware of the seed. Yet the seed remains alive; and when the earth is taken away, one again becomes aware of it, and the seed continues to grow ...

There is another metaphor. The sun shines continually; but when a cloud or mist comes between us and the sun, we cannot see its beams. Similarly, when the eye has some disease, or for some reason is covered, it cannot perceive the sunlight.

I have yet another metaphor. When a sculptor makes an image from a piece of wood or stone, he does not put the image onto the material. Rather, he cuts off pieces of the material which, as it were, are concealing and covering up the image. He gives nothing to the material; but he takes away material, digging and scraping and chopping, until the hidden image is revealed.

BECOMING THE SON

from *The Nobleman*

If my soul contemplates God, I am aware of my soul doing this; I not only know God, but I know that I know God. Some people believe that the true flower of contemplation, the true blessing, lies in this self-knowledge – the knowledge that I know God. If I had the joy of knowing God, and yet knew nothing about this knowledge, what kind of joy would it be? I do not agree with these people. Although it is true that self-knowledge is a blessing, the true blessing of God does not depend on self-knowledge.

The first thing on which divine blessing depends is that the soul should contemplate God, without any veil or barrier. In this experience the soul fulfils her being, she gains life, she draws energy from God himself. And in this experience she knows nothing of knowledge, or love, or anything at all. In the presence of God the soul becomes entirely and absolutely passive; she knows nothing except God. Yet when the soul stands back from the experience, and reflects upon the act of contemplation, she ceases to contemplate God, and reverts to a lower spiritual level …

Our inner selves receive and derive all spiritual

energy, all life and all happiness solely from God, by God and in God. We do not receive these things from knowing, contemplating or loving God, or from anything of that kind. Eternal life is to know God as the only true God, and yet not to know that one knows God.

How can the soul know that she knows God, without knowing herself? The soul truly contemplating God does not know herself at all, but knows only God; and this total contemplation of God is the root and ground of all divine blessing. Only outside contemplation can the soul know that she knows God, and also know herself.

Compare this with the gift of sight. There is one power by which we see, and another power by which we know and are aware that we see. It is true that the power by which we know and recognise sight is nobler and higher than the power of sight itself; this is because in nature the lower power precedes the higher. But God works from perfection downwards. Nature makes the adult from the child, and the hen from the egg; but God conceives the adult before the child, the hen before the egg. Nature makes the wood warm and hot, and only then makes it catch fire. But God first fashions every creature as a perfect conception, and then inserts the creature into time. In the same way God bestows the Holy Spirit on people, before bestowing the gifts of the Holy Spirit.

Thus on the one hand a blessing cannot exist unless the person being blessed is aware of contemplating God; yet on the other hand God cannot allow his blessing to depend on this. Those who make self-knowledge, rather than knowledge of God, their primary aim are wrong, and should be pitied. Feeling the heat of a fire, and the fire itself, are two entirely separate things, though they are close to one another in time and space. Equally, being aware of contemplation, and contemplation itself, are quite separate from one another ...

When I contemplate, I am seeking unity with myself by becoming unified with God; thus the self becomes absorbed into God. Subsequently I may return from this state of unity, and be aware that I have contemplated God ... It is surely nobler for the Son to be born within the soul, and for the soul thereby to know God, than for the soul merely to reflect on this.

IN PRAISE OF DETACHMENT

from *On Detachment*

I praise detachment more than love. The best thing about love is that it compels me to love God. Detachment, on the other hand, forces God to love me. It is much nobler that I should compel God to love me, than that I should compel myself to love God. The reason is that God can join and unite himself to me far more closely than I can unite myself to him. Detachment compels God to love me because everything loves to be in its own natural place. God's natural place is where there is harmony and purity; and detachment brings those qualities. Thus God must of necessity love a detached heart.

I also praise detachment more than love because love forces me to suffer all things for the sake of God, while detachment makes me receptive of nothing except God. It is far nobler to be receptive of nothing except God, than to suffer all things for the sake of God. When people suffer, they naturally focus their minds on the external causes of their suffering. But detachment has no external causes. Detachment is receptive of nothing except God because the process of something being received must involve a receptacle. Detachment creates a spiritual receptacle for God because it empties the heart of everything except God. And God is so simple and so gentle that he can easily enter a detached heart. Thus detachment is receptive of nothing except God.

As well as praising detachment above love, I praise detachment above humility. This is because humility can exist without detachment, but perfect detachment cannot exist without perfect humility. In fact perfect humility is inclined to destroy itself, whereas detachment leaves nothing to destroy. Thus humility leads towards detachment – and two virtues are always better than one.

I also praise detachment more than humility because perfect humility bows down before all creatures, treating all creatures as superior; in this way humility makes people focus on that which is external to themselves. But detachment remains within itself. Looking outwards can never be as noble as remaining within the self. Detachment does not bow down before anything, nor assert itself above anything. It wishes to be neither above nor below. It wishes to stand on its own, causing neither joy nor sorrow to anyone, wanting neither equality nor inequality with anyone, desiring nothing in particular. It does not wish to become anything. If people wish to become something, they cannot be detached, because detachment wishes to be nothing.

For this reason detachment is a burden to no one ...

You might ask: 'If detachment is so noble, what exactly is it?' Detachment is this: the spirit is unmoved by joy and sorrow, honour or disgrace; detachment is like a mountain of lead being buffeted by the wind. Those who have become immovable in this way are like God. For God to be divine he must be immovable; and from this comes his purity, his simplicity and his changelessness. Thus if people are to become like God, insofar as this is possible, they must acquire detachment. This will lead to purity; and purity will lead to simplicity; and simplicity will lead to changelessness. That is how people become like God. But this process depends on God's grace, since divine grace draws people away from worldly and transient concerns.

To be empty of worldly concerns is to be full of God; and to be full of worldly concerns is to be empty of God. For all eternity God has been detached and immovable. When God created heaven and earth and all that they contain, his immovable detachment was stirred as little as if creation had never occurred. Moreover, all the prayer and all the good works that people can perform in the world have as little effect on God's detachment as if those prayers and good works had never been performed. Thus God will not be more pleasant or more favourably disposed towards humans as a result of those prayers and good works. Indeed, I will go further: when the Son wished to become a human being, and was born in Bethlehem and died on the cross, this affected God's immovable detachment as little as if the Son had never become a human being.

You might reply: 'That means all our prayers and good works are vain, because God cannot be moved by such means. Yet we are told that God wishes us to ask for everything we need.' God, in his first eternal glance (if one can speak in such a way), saw how all events were to unfold; he discerned how each event would be caused; he looked upon every creature that would ever exist; and he saw when the Son would be born as a human being and suffer. He also saw the smallest prayer and tiniest good work that anyone was destined to perform, and considered what his response would be. He saw, for example, that a particular person will pray to him for a particular object tomorrow. But he will not answer that prayer tomorrow, because he has answered it from all eternity – from long before the person praying was even conceived. Conversely, if a particular prayer by a particular person is not sincere, God will not refuse that person now, because he refused from all eternity.

Thus in his first eternal glance God considered all things, and he decided all things; so he does nothing that he has not already chosen to do. God is always immovably detached ...

To understand detachment more fully, you need to recognise that there are two distinct aspects to human nature. The first is the outer person, which depends on the five senses; yet it operates by the power of the soul. The second is the inner person, the innermost part of human nature. Religious people who love God direct the soul towards the outer person only to the extent that the five senses require. The inner person is not concerned with the five senses, except to guide and lead them. The inner person takes care to prevent the five senses becoming enslaved to external objects, and thence going out of control.

Once the soul has dealt with the five senses, she devotes herself entirely to the inner person. And when she conceives a particular high and noble purpose, she draws back into herself all the energy she has lent to the five senses. This is why very holy people are often called senseless, or even mad; their focus of attention is an image within the mind, or even something transcending the mind which has no image. Indeed, God expects every holy person to love him with all the powers of the soul. There are some people who entirely dissipate the energy of the soul in outer matters; they direct themselves completely to the acquisition of wealth and pursuit of pleasure, and ignore the inner person.

The outer person may be suffering great pain and sorrow, but the inner person remains detached and immovable. Even in Jesus Christ there was an outer and an inner person, as there was in Mary. Whenever Christ or Mary spoke of outer feelings, their inner selves remained immovably detached. At the time of his crucifixion Christ expressed profound sorrow; and Mary wept profusely as she watched her son suffer. But even at this dire moment, they remained detached.

Let us use an analogy to describe this. I compare a door to the outer person, and the hinge on which the door swings to the inner person. The door moves every time someone opens and closes it; but the hinge does not move, remaining in one place.

A person may ask: 'What is the object of pure detachment?' I answer that pure detachment has no object. It aims at nothing. Or, more precisely, it aims to submit itself absolutely and without reserve to the will of God. Yet God's will cannot rule in all hearts; he can only rule if the heart is ready, or if he makes it ready through his grace. Thus God works differently in different hearts. We can find a parable of this in daily life. Imagine that you light an oven, and put inside it four pieces of dough, made of oats, barley, rye and wheat respectively. There is one heat in the oven, but it does not produce the same results in the dough. One piece turns into a fine loaf, the second is rough, and the third and fourth rougher still. The heat is not responsible for this, but the materials are. In the same way God does not achieve the same results in all human hearts; his achievements depend on their readiness and receptivity. Indeed, he will achieve very little in a heart filled with worldly lusts and desires.

Thus, if the heart is to be transformed, it must make itself ready. It must aim at nothing; and then it will have the highest possible goal. When the heart is truly directed towards nothing, it will be truly receptive towards God. We can find a further parable. Imagine that I want to write on a wax tablet, and find some extremely fine words already written on it. But if I am to fulfil my desire to write, I must delete all those fine words. In the same way, when God wishes to write on my heart, everything that is already on my heart, however fine it may be, must first be deleted. Then God can do what he wants with my heart. Thus the object of the detached heart must be nothing.

What, then, is the prayer of the detached heart? The answer is that purity and detachment cannot pray. Prayer means asking God for something to be given, or something to be taken away. But the detached heart does not ask for anything at all, nor does it wish to be rid of anything. Therefore it is free from all prayer – apart from praying to be unified with God. The prayer of detachment is submission to God.

DOING AND BEING

―――――◆―――――

from *Talks of Instruction 4*

People never need to think about what they ought to be doing; they should think about what they are. If people are truly good, then their actions will radiate goodness. If people are just, their actions will radiate justice. Holiness is not based on actions, but on being. Actions do not make people holy; but holiness sanctifies actions. Even if actions appear to be holy, they cannot make the people doing those actions holy. But if the people themselves are holy, then even sleeping and eating become holy.

JOYFUL BURDENS

———◆———

from *Talks of Instruction 18*

You do not need to worry whether the food you eat
or the clothes you wear are too good for you. What
matters is that your mind is above such things.
Nothing should move your mind to joy or love other
than God; your mind should not be concerned with
lower matters. Why? Because the garments you are
wearing cannot affect your spiritual devotion. The
inner quality of your devotion makes any garment
seem appropriate. So you should feel equally happy
and comfortable in any kind of garment. The same
applies to food: you should be equally happy with
any kind of food. And the same even applies to
friends, relations and any other aspect of your life. Let
God give, and let God take away.

If you surrender yourself totally to God, you will
accept with joy and gratitude any burden that he may
put upon you, be it the contempt of others, physical
hardship or any other kind of suffering. You will
allow God to lead you, rather than lead yourself.
Learn whatever God teaches you, and apply what you
learn; then all will go well for you. At times you may
be treated with respect, and enjoy good health; at

other times you may be treated badly, and endure poor health. At times you are permitted to eat normally; at other times you are required to fast. But at all times give thanks to God.

Since great spiritual profit comes from suffering, God allows his friends to suffer; he does not want to deprive them of any good thing. Nonetheless he sometimes relieves his friends of all pain, and permits them to enjoy much earthly pleasure. He does this when he is satisfied that their wills have become good and righteous.

So long as God is happy with what is happening to you, be content. If with your whole will you belong to God, you will not worry about your material circumstances or the work you are doing. You will not be concerned with food or clothing. You will not try to win respect with pious words or gestures. And you will be quite willing to accept the customs and traditions of the people around you; you will adapt yourself to others without complaint.

GOD IN ALL PEOPLE AND THINGS

from *Talks of Instruction 6*

If God is in you, then he remains in you wherever you go. When you walk down the street, or visit friends, God is in you – just as much as when you are in church, in the desert or in a monastic cell. So long as God, and God alone, is in you nothing or no one can hinder you. Why? Because when the mind is totally fixed on God, then all things become nothing but God.

You carry God wherever you go, and in every action you perform. Indeed, all your actions are performed by God; this is because he is the cause of your actions and is responsible for them. Thus when you concentrate your mind purely and simply on God, he is working in and through you; so neither your circumstances, nor the people around you, can hinder you. You will aim for nothing and seek nothing except to unite your endeavours to God's; and you will seek no reward except the knowledge of doing God's will. And just as God cannot be disturbed by complexity and difficulty, in the same way nothing will upset you or disturb your thoughts. In God all complexity is simplicity, all difficulty is blessing.

You should see God in all things; and you should constantly remind yourself that God is in your mind, in your actions, and in your heart. To do this you need to keep watch over your mind. When you go out into the crowd and into the clamour of the world, keep the same mood that you have in church or in your cell. You should not regard all activities and all places as equally noble or worthwhile. On the contrary, it is better to pray than to spin; and a church is an easier context for prayer than a road. But in all places and in all activities you should be tranquil and serene, and keep your mind fixed firmly on God. In fact if you are firm in this way, no one can take your mind away from God.

POSSESSING THE TRUE GOD

from *Talks of Instruction 6*

How can we possess God? Possession of God depends on the heart: the heart must honestly strive for God. It does not depend merely on thinking about God. In fact it is impossible for the mind constantly to think about God; it would be too arduous. Moreover, if we think too much about God there is a danger that we create in our minds an imaginary God; and this God fades away as our thoughts fade. We want to possess the real God, who is far above human thought. This God does not fade away — although we can turn our back on him.

When we possess God, we look at the world around us in a godly manner. We see the light of God shining in all things; all things have the flavour and form of God. Equally, the light of God shines in us; people looking at us can see God dwelling within us.

The possession of God can be illustrated in parables. If you are parched, you can still do and think about other things apart from your thirst. But whatever you do and think, whoever you are with, and whatever your aims, the idea of drinking does not leave you. And the greater the thirst, the more intense and persistent is the idea of drinking. Similarly, if you love something with great passion, such that nothing else you taste or touch feels good, then whatever you are planning or doing, and whatever company you are in, the love for that object will not die. You find the image of what you love in everything you see; and the object of your love is always in your thoughts. You know that the object of your love is your only source of peace.

Those who possess God value things more highly than their intrinsic worth, because they perceive God in them. Careful attention to the inner person is required to attain this spiritual state, leading to a profound understanding and knowledge of the people and things that God has created. You cannot attain this knowledge by fleeing from the world and living in solitude. Yet this knowledge requires you to cultivate an inner solitude, whoever you are with, and wherever you are. You must learn mentally to break through the surface of people and things, and to grasp God within them, picturing his presence.

Let us use another parable. If you want to learn and master the skill of writing, you must practise frequently; and you must persist, even when the work is arduous, and you are in despair. You have to concentrate on the letters of the alphabet in turn, impressing each one on your mind, and forming each one with your hand. Eventually you will find yourself able to write fluently and freely. The same kind of diligence is required to play a musical instrument, or perform any other kind of art. Every form of artistic expression depends on the individual having the necessary skill.

In the same way, if you want God to live within you and to transform you, and if you want the presence of God to radiate from you without effort, then your heart must learn to strive for God without distraction. This skill can only be acquired with great diligence and concentration.

WRAPPED IN GOD

———————◆———————

from *Talks of Instruction 11*

We know that God's love for us is constant. But often in our hearts we feel he has gone away, and we miss him. What should we do at such times? Recollect how you were, and how you acted, when he felt close; and act in the same way now. Indeed you should do this when you are in any kind of distress. The best time to find God is when God seems most distant …

In effect I am saying that you should surrender your will to God at all times and in all circumstances. Without surrendering our will to God, we can achieve nothing. But when we truly surrender our will to him, and renounce all things for his sake, both inner and outer, then we have achieved everything that it is possible to achieve.

Whether or not they are aware of it, most people are very reluctant to surrender their will to God. They yearn for some particular emotion, or to enjoy a particular way of life, or to receive some particular blessing. But this is self-will. You should surrender yourself to God in all respects, and then not concern yourself with how he chooses to use you. Of course, there are countless people who pass their lives without ever surrendering their wills to God. But you should aspire to true perfection, in which you follow the way of God without deviation. The more you surrender to God, the closer you come to him. It is better to say one prayer in an attitude of true surrender, than a thousand prayers without that attitude. It is better to take one step with that attitude, than to make a pilgrimage to Jerusalem without it.

Those who have surrendered their will are wrapped in God, so that when others touch them they are touching God. Such people are totally in God, and God is around them – just as my head is my head, and my head is around my head.

THE SUFFERING OF GOD

from *Talks of Instruction 11*

If I suffer greatly, and if that suffering comes from God, then God suffers first. If I entrust any kind of suffering to God, even some quite trivial discomfort, it will affect God immeasurably more than it affects me; it will be far worse for God than for me.

If God suffers for the sake of some blessing he has destined for you, and if you are willing to share that suffering as he requires, then you shall become godlike. He may require you to be treated with contempt, to endure the bitterness of betrayal, or be cast into deep depression. So long as the suffering is sent by God, it will mould and bend you into his image.

Thus I ask you to look for God in bitterness, just as much as in sweetness. And you should desire divine bitterness as much as you desire divine sweetness.

BEING IN HEAVEN ON EARTH

————◆————

from *Talks of Instruction 7*

We should each use our reason to keep watch over our own thoughts and over our devotion to God. In this way we shall learn to perceive God in all things. Servants, who are expecting their lord to return late at night, lie awake waiting for him; and whenever they hear a noise, even the slightest sound, they look to see if it is him. In the same way we should be looking out for God. This requires great diligence; our mind and our energy must be wholly devoted to the task. But the reward is great: we shall experience great joy in seeing God everywhere, in an equal degree.

We shall also find God in our most menial daily tasks. Certainly tasks vary in the skill and effort needed; but if each task is undertaken with equanimity, then all will be equally good. Indeed, when we perform a menial task with the same spiritual care as we perform our worship, then God will shine in us equally in both. Of course God cannot shine in us when our work is motivated by greed or malice; but all normal work in the world can be offered to God in the same way that we offer prayers.

If God is present to us in all we do, and our reason ensures that we are constantly mindful of God, then we shall know true peace; we shall be in heaven, even while living on earth.

KNOWING ETERNITY

from *Talks of Instruction 14*

There are two kinds of knowledge about eternal life. The first is what God himself says to individuals, announcing it to them through an angel, or revealing it in some special way. This happens rarely and to few people.

The second kind of knowledge is far better and more valuable. It is experienced by all loving souls. From the love and affection you have for God, you fully and completely trust God, knowing that God loves all his creatures without distinction.

Even if all your friends turned against you, swearing hostility to you, and even if God himself seemed to turn against you, you would not stop trusting him. Love cannot mistrust; it trusts all that is good. If you trust God there is no need to speak to him and plead with him; you know that he is your friend, and you can rely on his devotion. Though you love him totally, his love for you is far greater than your love for him; he is love itself.

MOTIVE AND ACTION

from *Talks of Instruction 10*

You should not be afraid of anything, so long as your will is good; nor should you be upset if you do not achieve your aims in your work. If you have genuine good will, you can never stray far from the path of virtue, because virtue depends on good will. Indeed everything that is truly good in this life depends on good will. If you have good will, you will lack nothing that is precious: you will not lack love, humility or any other quality. People of good will attain whatever they desire; neither God nor any of his creatures can take it away from them – provided that the desire is godly, and that God is present in it ...

If my will is evil, even if I have never committed an evil act, then I am guilty of sin. If I wholeheartedly want to destroy the entire world, I am guilty of that terrible sin – even though I cannot enact my will.

To put the same point another way, I can do all things by my will. I can bear all the hardships of the human race; I can feed all the poor; I can do the work of a hundred – I can accomplish whatever I can imagine. In the sight of God, it is a person's will, not the power to act, that matters. No one can take your will away from you, or hinder you from pointing your will in whichever direction you choose. To want to do something as soon as possible, and to have done it, are the same in God's eyes.

THE VALUE OF WEAKNESS

from *Talks of Instruction 9*

Consider two types of people. Those who belong to the first type are morally and spiritually strong, so they are not tempted to do wrong. Those who belong to the second type are prey to external influences. They are easily stirred to anger or pride, and they are beset by greed and lust. Yet in their inner selves they have become steadfast and immovable. They will not give way to their evil desires, and vigorously resist temptation. Thus despite their natural weakness, they do not fall into sin. This second type of person is far more praiseworthy than the first type: through struggling with their weakness, they have become perfect in virtue.

The inclination to sin is not sin. But the will to sin, and the will to anger, is sin. Indeed if you were wise, and if you had the power to choose, you would want to have an inclination to sin. Without this inclination you would not have the opportunity to become firm and resolute; you would not learn to be vigilant; and you could not acquire the honour of fighting and defeating evil. The battle against evil brings great virtue and reward.

BAD AND GOOD GUILT

from *Talks of Instruction 13*

There are two kinds of repentance: the first is temporal and earthly; the second is divine and heavenly. Temporal repentance plunges the soul deeper and deeper into remorse: it sinks into the mire of misery and despair. This kind of repentance only causes pain; nothing good comes of it.

Divine repentance is quite different. As soon as you feel remorse, you lift your thoughts immediately up to God, and with unshakeable trust you place yourself in his hands. You express to God your wish to renounce all sin for ever. Soon you feel a wonderful sense of security, which produces spiritual joy. This raises the soul out of all pain and sorrow, and binds it to God. The weaker you are, and the worse your sin, the more you want to bind yourself with cords of love to God, in whom there is neither weakness nor sin. And the closer to God you grow, the less attractive sin becomes, making your repentance complete.

This process shows that you must be honest about your sin, giving it full weight. In this way God can forgive it completely, and drive sin away from you.

FALSE AND TRUE PENANCE

———◆———

from *Talks of Instruction 16*

Many people think they need to perform many external acts, such as fasting, walking barefoot, and other things of this kind – which are generally called works of penance. But true and proper penance, which brings the greatest improvement to your life, consists in renouncing everything in yourself and your attachments that is not godly. Penance consists of turning away from worldly attachments towards God, prompted by a deep desire and devotion for him.

This penance means that the mind is constantly focused on God. And you should engage in any activity that helps you to focus your mind on God. Equally, if particular activities – be it fasting, vigils, spiritual reading, or anything else – hinder you, then give them up without delay or anxiety. God is not concerned with what precisely you do, but about the effects of what you do on your state of mind and soul. It is not what we do that matters, but our spiritual and mental attitude. God knows what you are doing, and he simply desires that he should be your ultimate goal; that is sufficient. The more you aim at him, the greater will be your reward.

THE MEANING OF LOVE

from *Talks of Instruction 10*

There are two aspects of love: the first is the essential, inner nature of love; the second is the work and expression of love. The essence of love is in the will; those who have a stronger and better will have stronger and better love. But one person cannot tell whether another person has much love or little love. Love lies deeply hidden within the soul – as does God himself. To love is to have the will to love.

The expression of love takes many forms. It may take the form of devout worship, or of joyfully singing God's praise. But do not assume that all worship and singing is prompted by love; people may worship God and sing hymns because they enjoy doing so. In other words, the desire to worship may come from heaven, via the soul, or it may come from the senses ... Yet worship is not the highest expression of love. Imagine yourself in a state of ecstatic joy during an act of worship; and you were called on to perform an act of charity, such as giving a bowl of soup to a hungry stranger. It would be more loving to desist from the worship, and feed the stranger.

THE FREE MIND

———◆———

from *Talks of Instruction 2*

The most powerful and effective prayer is the prayer that comes from a free mind. Indeed, praying in freedom is the most valuable way we can use our time. The more free our prayer is, the more worthy, useful, noble and perfect it becomes. A free mind has the power to perform all things.

What is a free mind? A free mind is one that is not perplexed by anything or attached to anything. It is not tied to any particular way of life; nor does it consider its own advantage. A free mind concentrates only on the will of God, renouncing its own will. A free mind wants to do whatever God wants, knowing that God is the source of its strength and energy.

A free mind prays in such a way that the entire body and the five senses are all directed to God. And it does not cease to pray until it is totally unified with God, and is in his presence.

LACK OF INHIBITIONS

❖

from *Talks of Instruction 21*

You should learn to be free and uninhibited in all your activities. But for a mature person, learning to be free is an unusual and even frightening challenge. Great enthusiasm is needed; and this can only be engendered if you are constantly aware of God in all situations, so that his light can shine brightly. You also need to be very zealous, in two particular ways. First, you should be inwardly self-reliant, so that your heart is not disturbed by external impressions and images; you must not let your freedom be compromised by what is outside you — external images have no place inside you. Secondly, you should not allow yourself to be distracted, exhausted and enslaved by internal images, such as idle fancies, or by foolish emotions such as personal pride; you should use all your spiritual strength to combat these spiritual snares.

Now you might reply: 'I must look outwards if I am to be free in my outward activities, otherwise I shall be able to do nothing.' This is true. But a mature person has control over the external images that come into the mind, so the inner self remains free.

This means that you must train your mind to be devoted entirely to God, so that he occupies your inner self. The more fully God is present within you, the more indifferent you will be to external things – and so the more freedom you will enjoy. But if God is not present your inner self will be overwhelmed and imprisoned by external things. If God has been driven out of you by external desires and passions, then you must exert great energy to control and suppress those desires.

The fact is that God's natural place is in your inner self; and your inner self belongs to God. When the inner self is enslaved to external things, then you lose self-reliance and you become spiritually deformed. All your best endeavours are hindered, and you can achieve nothing. Thus true freedom requires constant vigilance.

Thus we have a paradox: freedom depends on self-control. And this self-control depends on acquiring steady and good habits. If inexperienced and untrained people try to behave like experienced ones, they destroy themselves and achieve nothing. But if you first wean yourself from bad ways of thinking and acting, and estrange yourself from them, then you will be free in all you do. You will no longer feel anxious about yourself. The inexperienced person, who tries to act freely, merely becomes a slave to food, drink or whatever.

AMPLE TIME

from *Talks of Instruction 21* and *22*

Time never seems too short to people of good will. When the will is directed towards goodness, then it will accomplish all that it should accomplish. This is the same whether the time available is a day or a thousand years. The person of good will always does precisely what God wants …

You should only try to do one thing at a time; you cannot do everything at once. Yet in each thing that you do you should apprehend all things. If you are constantly changing from one activity to another, always wanting to do something different, you are abandoning the path God has chosen for you, and moving on to other people's paths. And this will make your mind and soul very unstable.

People in religious orders are just as prone to flitting from one activity to another as those outside; and some are constantly wanting to change from one order to another. You should simply follow one way of life, and stick to it; all that matters is that God has destined you for that way of life.

SPIRITUAL PARADOXES

from *Talks of Instruction 17*

It is often better to avoid becoming anxious than to fast. It is often better to remain silent than to risk saying something that would hurt another person. It is often easier to hear a very full account of one's faults, than to endure a single contemptuous word. It is often harder to be alone in a crowd than in a desert. It is often harder to give up a small thing than a great one, and to undertake a small task than a great one. All this points to our weakness, but the weaker we are, the stronger God is on our behalf.

from *Talks of Instruction 17*

People are sometimes overcome with timidity, because the lives of Jesus Christ and the saints were so strict and arduous; they feel they cannot imitate their example, and nor do they want to imitate it. They regard themselves as utterly different in character from Jesus and the saints, and so consider themselves very far from God and unable to follow him.

No one should take this attitude. People should not think of themselves as far from God, merely because they are guilty of some sin or are weak in some way, or for any other reason. If at any time your sins drive you away from God, so you feel distant from him, you should still know that God is near you. You can do yourself great damage if you try to remove yourself from God. Although you may go far away from him, he remains close to you; if he cannot stay beside you, he is still only just outside the door.

Do not worry about the strictness of Christ's style of life. You are called to imitate him not in a slavish manner, but by following the vocation for which he has destined you. Different people are called in different ways. You may well find that your way does not involve great hardship and austerity. Indeed external hardships in themselves are quite unimportant; they only matter if God has called you to them – and he would only do this if he had given you the strength to endure them. If you do not feel yourself called to any particular hardships, be content and do not fret about it.

You might say: 'If these austerities are so unimportant, why did so many saints inflict them on themselves?' The reason is that for some people hardships and austerities are necessary as a means of attaining salvation. But God has not restricted human salvation to a particular way of life. What one person needs, another does not. Many paths lead to God, and all are equally good. The fact that one path leads to God does not mean that others do not. People do great harm when they criticise others on different paths, saying that their efforts are wasted. These critics are confusing their own personal needs and preferences with that which is right and good. One person should never criticise the religious practices of another; what matters is the spiritual devotion that motivates those practices.

You should be true to your own way of devotion; and you should rejoice in all the other ways.

FURTHER READING

A readily available translation of Eckhart's work is *Meister Eckhart: Selected Writings*, published by Penguin (1994) and edited by O. Davies, who has also published a book *about* Eckhart: *Meister Eckhart: Mystical Theologian* (SPCK, 1991).

Element Books has published a fuller version, *Meister Eckhart: German Sermons & Treatises*, edited by M. O'C. Walshe (3 volumes, 1987, not all in print in 1998), and Bear & Co. has published *Meditations with Meister Eckhart* by M. Fox (1983).